50 Day Easter Study Guide

50 Days Before Easter Study Guide

by

Bruce Buckingham

Risky Living Ministries, Inc.

50 Days Before Easter Study Guide
By Bruce Buckingham

Published by Risky Living Ministries, Inc.
3901 Hield Road NW
Palm Bay, FL 32907

www.RiskyLivingMinistries.com

Risky Living Ministries is dedicated to preserving the
teachings and life works of Jamie Buckingham.

Cover photo of "Christ in the Sanctuary," Saint Isaac's
Cathedral, St. Petersburg, Russia, by Bruce Buckingham

ISBN-13: 978-1976272950

Foreword

Are you searching for a great daily video devotional? Welcome to *50 Days Before Easter* with Jamie Buckingham, a unique concept for individual or group devotions.

This study guide is specifically tailored to be used alongside Jamie Buckingham's acclaimed video series. The videos are designed to be viewed daily during the seven weeks leading up to Easter Sunday, but they can be watched anytime.

During each daily six-minute video, Jamie will lead you through the Holy Land, following the footsteps of Jesus, from Galilee to the Holy City of Jerusalem. Through his unique teaching style, his familiarity with the land of Israel, and his deep knowledge of the Bible, Jamie will help draw you closer to the Lord and discover more about God's wonderful plan for your life.

To fully use this study guide, it is suggested you first watch each day's video in its entirety. Then go back and watch it again, listening closely for the answers to the questions in this book. Write your answers directly in the study guide. The answers to all the questions are listed in the back.

Let God speak to you from the land of the Bible and from the life of Jesus in this daily devotional, as Jamie helps you to prepare your heart to celebrate the great day of the Resurrection of our Lord.

View the videos online at: www.50DaysBeforeEaster.com.

Bruce Buckingham
Palm Bay, Florida

Jamie Buckingham

Day 49 — Sunday before Lent — *"Introit"*

This first video is the introduction to the series of devotional videos known as *50 Days Before Easter*. In this series, Jamie Buckingham goes into detail about the life of Christ, including His message, His heritage, and His lifestyle, to give us a perfectly clear understanding of who this man, Jesus, was—and is.

1. What does the term *Lent* mean? _____

_____

_____

2. What does the traditional 40 days of Lent symbolize? _____

_____

_____

3. What does the term *quinquagayseema* mean? _____

_____

4. What is the purpose of Lent? _____

_____

_____

_____

Day 48 — *Dead Sea Scrolls*

In this devotional, filmed on location near the Dead Sea in Israel, Jamie describes how the Dead Sea Scrolls were discovered and recalls the baptism of Jesus.

As you approach this Lenten season, remember: you are part of a great process of bringing the kingdom of God to this world.

1. What year were the Dead Sea scrolls discovered?

_____

2. What do the Dead Sea Scrolls contain? _____

_____

3. What was one of the tenets of the Essenes mentioned in the video? _____

_____

4. Who is perhaps the most well-known Essene?

_____

5. Why did Jesus insist John the Baptist baptism Him?

_____

6. Why is Psalm 2:7 so important in reference to Jesus' baptism? _____

_____

Day 47 — *God's Rest*

For the children of Israel, the Negev Desert was the scene of a great deal of unrest. It is where they wandered for 40 years following their exodus from Egypt under Moses' leadership and after stopping short of the Promised Land.

Certainly, that is not the destination that God wants for any of us. We need to quiet our hearts and spirits in order to receive God's rest and peace. Only those who obey God will find rest. The rest of God is offered to all people through Jesus.

1. The Negev Desert is also known by what biblical names? _____

_____

2. What is significant about the date Oct. 29, 1956, for Israel? _____

_____

3. What happened during the week of June 5, 1967?

_____

_____

4. How do we best find rest in God? _____

_____

_____

Day 46 — *Repentance and Fasting*

Today, many Christians will celebrate Ash Wednesday and the beginning of the season of Lent. It is a wonderful season of walking with God and making a fresh commitment to Jesus Christ. The ashes many receive on their foreheads today are a symbol of repentance, humility, fasting and prayer.

1. What is the first day of Lent commonly called?

_____

2. What do the ashes of Lent symbolize? _____

_____

3. What is considered the most sacred place in the world for Jews? _____

4. How long before the coming of Christ did Solomon build the original Temple? _____

5. During the years the Jews were scattered across the earth, a time called the Diaspora, who took over the city of Jerusalem? _____

6. What Biblical artifact do Muslims say is located in the Dome of the Rock? _____

_____

7. How should we fast? _____

_____

Day 45 — *New Growth*

Israel has been a land of strife and conflict since the days of Abraham. Few nations on Earth have been through as many wars, suffered as much grief, or seen as much bloodshed. Yet, Israel is a blessed and highly favored nation.

Terrorists think they can destroy Israel, just as Satan, 2,000 years ago, thought he could stop the Messiah from saving the world by nailing Him to a cross. "Such is the price of being chosen."

1. Why do many Jews believe they are persecuted?

_____

_____

2. When Jews began to return to the Holy Land in 1948, what was one of the first things they did to help restore the land? _____

_____

_____

3. What is the primary water source for the nation of Israel? _____

_____

4. Which Old Testament prophet said, "There is hope for a tree"? _____

Day 44 — *Two Kings: Herod and Jesus*

When it came to worldly wealth, King Herod had it all. Money, power, possessions—there was nothing he wanted or lacked, except, perhaps, inner peace.

On the other hand, as the Son of God, Jesus didn't have many earthly possessions; yet, He was a man of peace and love and was filled with inner contentment. Herod had no regard for human life. In stark contrast, Jesus came to save the world.

1. Who was king in Israel when Jesus was born?

_____

2. To what religious group did Herod belong?

_____

3. Which prophet from the Old Testament prophesied the Messiah would be born in Bethlehem? _____

_____

4. How many sons did Herod have, and what were their names? _____

_____

_____

_____

Day 43 — *Angels*

It is impossible to think about Jesus' life on Earth without thinking about the angels who surrounded Him, ministered to Him, and protected Him.

This devotional recounts the many times angels were present and active throughout the life of Christ.

1. When and where did the greatest angel visitation known to man take place? _____

_____

2. What does the Greek term for angel, *angelus*, mean?

_____

3. What are the three main roles that angels perform?

_____

_____

4. Why does the Apostle Paul warn us to be careful about turning away strangers? _____

_____

5. What did the angels say to those who came to the empty tomb of Jesus? _____

_____

Day 42 — *Overcoming Temptation*

Throughout the life of Jesus, Satan was constantly attempting to turn Christ from His true mission on Earth. Every time, Satan failed.

Jesus is still victorious today! As Christians filled with the Holy Spirit, we, too, have authority to rebuke Satan, and he will flee from us.

1. How far below sea level is the Dead Sea? _____

2. Where did Jesus go and how long was He there, following His baptism in the Jordan River? _____

_____

3. What was the inauguration of Jesus' public ministry? _____

_____

4. What happened when Jesus came up out of the water during His baptism? _____

_____

5. What were the three temptations of Jesus in the Judean wilderness? _____

_____

_____

Day 41— *Messiah's Throne*

Many Jews believed the Messiah would come as a "thundering prophet," like Jeremiah. Others believed He would be like Moses, or Judas the Maccabee.

As Jesus' crucifixion drew nearer, the disciples began to realize that Jesus was not the Messiah the rabbis had taught them to expect. He was more like the Messiah prophesied by the prophet Isaiah.

1. What does the term *Messiah* mean in Hebrew?

_____

2. What is the Greek word for "anointed one?"

_____

3. What did the ancient Jews believe the Messiah would do for them? _____

_____

4. What is the highest city in Israel?

_____

5. What is the sacred rock on Mt. Meron called?

_____

6. How long before the birth of Jesus did the prophet Isaiah prophesy His coming? _____

Day 40 — *Deliverance*

In Mark 9, a man whose son had an unclean spirit came to Jesus' disciples, asking them to cast the spirit out. The disciples could not do it. Then the man brought the boy to Jesus, and with a single rebuke, Jesus drove the demon out.

The disciples talked about power and authority; but when it came down to doing anything at that time, they were helpless. This passage of scripture draws a great parallel to many of today's churches, which are helpless without the power and authority of Jesus.

1. Which three disciples witnessed the transfiguration of Jesus alongside Moses and Elijah? _____

_____

2. What did the disciples want to do after they saw the transfiguration? _____

_____

3. How did Jesus deliver the young deaf and dumb boy of the evil spirit?

_____

4. Jesus didn't come only to make sure we are able to get to heaven. For what other purpose did He come?

_____

Day 39 — *The Sermon on the Mount*

Jesus' sermon found in the book of Matthew was not meant for the masses that had gathered to hear Him preach. It was, instead, a simple teaching session for His disciples. Over time "the Beatitudes" have become one of the most famous passages in the Bible, as Jesus teaches what the kingdom of God is really about.

1. Where is the Sermon on the Mount believed to have taken place? _____

2. When Jesus gave this great sermon, as recorded in Matthew, to whom was He speaking? _____

_____

3. What does the term *blessed* mean? _____

4. What did Jesus teach His disciples the kingdom of God was really about? _____

_____

5. Why will the true followers of Jesus always be persecuted by the world? _____

_____

6. What town was Jesus referencing when He said, "A city on a hill cannot be hidden"? _____

_____

Day 38 — *Spiritual Authority*

When Jesus began His public ministry, demons trembled when He came near. His very presence stirred up the demonic spirits operating in the unseen world— a world with which Jesus was familiar.

Before He ascended into heaven, Jesus told His disciples, "I'm going to give you the same power and authority over demons that I have, when the Holy Spirit comes upon you." We're not subject to evil spirits—they are subject to us.

1. Where was Jesus when He called His first disciples?

_____

2. What is the name of the mountainous area annexed by Israel from Syria in 1967 during the Six-Day War?

_____

3. Before leading a rebellion in heaven and being cast out, Lucifer was one of three archangels. Who are the other two? _____

4. Where did demons originate? _____

_____

5. Who gives us power today to cast out evil spirits?

_____

Day 37 — *Casting Out Demons*

In Matthew 8, Jesus took authority over a legion of demons that has possessed a man. Jesus cast the demons into a herd of swine,

Today, people who are demon-possessed can be set free by the same authority. We should remember the power Jesus Christ gives us over evil spirits.

In Ephesians 6 the Apostle Paul points out that our struggle is not against flesh and blood, but against principalities and powers, against the rulers of the darkness of this world. These evil powers have no authority over us, unless we allow it.

1. In 67 A.D., how many Jews died by the Roman sword in Gamla? _____

2. What happened to all the demons when Jesus told them to come out of the man living in the tombs?

_____

_____

3. Paul said our struggle is not against flesh and blood but against what? _____

_____

4. How are Christians told to deal with demons? _____

_____

Day 36 — *Hope for the Hopeless*

Jesus was a man of deep compassion. He cared not only for the physical needs of the people He met, but also for their souls—for the deep hurts that lay far beneath the surface of their physical bodies.

When Jesus touched and healed the lepers, for instance, He was touching more than their sick bodies; He was reaching into their very souls and healing them completely.

1. In the days of Jesus, what was the disease of leprosy known as? _____

_____

2. According to Levitical law, how were lepers to be treated? _____

_____

3. What laws did Jesus override when dealing with lepers? _____

_____

Day 35 — *Born Again*

Being born again is the first step in our walk with Jesus.

Once, when a religious man asked Jesus what he had to do to be saved, Jesus declared, "You must be born again." According to Jesus, it was not enough to keep all the laws, as the Jewish leaders taught; you must enter into a relationship with God—a relationship that goes far beyond following rules, acting religious, or playing church games.

1. To whom did Jesus say, "You must be born again"?

_____

2. What was the name of the ruling group of religious leaders in Jerusalem? _____

_____

3. When Jesus spoke of being "born again," what did He mean? _____

_____

_____

4. How do you become "born again"? _____

_____

_____

Day 34 — *Solitude and Prayer*

Two things seemed to be especially important to Jesus: solitude and prayer. The Bible says that while large crowds followed Jesus, He often withdrew to lonely places to pray in solitude.

Prayer is a two-way conversation with God. It is not a formula or a posture we take. When you pray, find a solitary place and talk to God as a child talks to his father. Then, listen to what God has to say back to you.

1. How long were the Zealots able to hold out against the Romans at Masada? _____

2. What event in Jewish history was marked by the fall of Masada in 73 A.D.?_____

_____

3. According to Luke, where did Jesus like to go to pray? _____

_____

4. What is prayer? _____

_____

_____

Day 33 — *Defeat and Victory*

In many instances in the Bible, defeat went before victory. Elijah knew this. So did Jesus, who was crucified before His glorious resurrection.

Whether we're experiencing the depths of defeat or the highs of victory, we know that God is in control. For the followers of Jesus, defeat is never final. Ultimate victory is always just around the corner.

1. With the exception of His trip into Egypt as an infant, what is the farthest distance Jesus traveled?

_____

2. Where did the prophet Elijah have a showdown with the 300 priests of Baal? _____

_____

3. What did the small cloud seen by Elijah's servant represent to Israel? _____

_____

4. When Jezebel sought to kill Elijah, where did he flee to? _____

5. When Elijah asked God to take his life, what did God do instead? _____

_____

Day 32 — *Clouds of Blessing*

In the Bible, the appearance of clouds often closely correlates with those times when God reveals Himself.

Moses encountered clouds when God gave him the Law at the top of Mount Sinai. The morning Jesus was crucified, a dark cloud appeared; but out of that cloud of despair came life three days later.

Biblically speaking, clouds are a sign that God is present and at work.

1. In the Bible, what is rain considered a sign of? _____

_____

2. What are clouds often connected to in the Scriptures? _____

_____

3. What are perhaps the most significant clouds in all of history? _____

_____

_____

Day 31 — *The Good Shepherd*

In John 10, Jesus said, "I am the Good Shepherd. The Good Shepherd lays down His life for the sheep."

God calls us as believers to lay down our lives for God's sheep. This can be done in many ways, including service to others and giving to those less fortunate.

Find someone who needs you, and be a shepherd to them for Jesus' sake.

1. What is Israel's number one source of revenue?

_____

2. What did Jesus liken His ministry to? _____

_____

3. How can we "lay down our lives for our friends"?

_____

_____

4. What did poet Elizabeth Barrett Browning consider to be a success for her life? _____

_____

Day 30 — *The Watch Tower*

In Matthew 21, Jesus taught the parable of the vineyard and the vinedressers. In the parable, the vinedressers grew greedy, attempting to keep the fruits of the vineyard to themselves.

Each of us has a sacred obligation to take care of the field where we've been placed. Today, take a few minutes to check out your field—whether it's your job, your family, your church, your money, or your faith. We are tenant managers. Let's never forget Who owns the field.

1. What was the purpose of the watch tower in the field of harvest? _____

_____

2. What does the name Jesus used for Himself, "son of man," mean? _____

3. What does the term "husbandman" mean? _____

_____

4. As tenant managers of God's "fields," what is our obligation? _____

_____

Day 29 — *Dominion*

This devotional, filmed at the Sea of Galilee, recounts the story of Jesus calming the sea as He and His disciples were crossing to the opposite side. Jesus took dominion over the winds and the waves, commanding them to be calm.

That same authority is available to all believers, if we will only walk with Christ and believe. Jesus came to restore dominion over this world.

1. What happened when Jesus and His disciples crossed the Sea of Galilee from Capernaum to Gadara?

_____

2. How far below sea level is the Sea of Galilee?

_____

3. How did Jesus speak to the high winds and waves on the water? _____

4. What does it mean to have dominion? _____

_____

5. When do we take dominion over Satan? _____

_____

Day 28 — *Feeding the Multitudes*

The multiplication of two fish and five loaves into enough food to feed more than 5,000 people is one of the most remarkable of all Jesus' miracles. It not only shows Christ's compassion for the wellbeing of people; it also displays the unlimited resources available to us as His followers.

1. How did John the Baptist die? _____

_____

2. How many people were present when Jesus determined they needed to be fed? _____

3. What spiritual principle is expressed in the feeding of the multitude? _____

_____

4. How much food did Jesus start with to feed the people? _____

_____

5. How much was left over after all were fed? _____

_____

Day 27 — *Christ or Caesar*

In biblical times, Caesars—Roman kings—came and went. When one Caesar passed on, he was soon forgotten, as another one took his place.

But Jesus, who suffered a horrible death at the hands of the Romans, lives on, empowering people through His spirit to spread the kingdom of God throughout the world. His influence is more evident today than ever before.

God does not need more Caesars. He needs good men and women who will not deny His Son when faced with the "lions" of this world.

1. Who built Caesarea-by-the-Sea, and how long did it take? _____

_____

2. Why did the Romans kill Christians and Jews in the coliseums? _____

_____

3. What does the Bible say about those who die for their faith? _____

_____

Day 26 — *The Hem of His Garment*

In Luke 8, the story is told of a woman who had a "hemorrhage" for 12 years that could not be healed by physicians. The woman thought to herself, "If only I can touch the fringe of Jesus' garment, I will be healed."

If we are sick, suffering, or hurting, we too can be healed, if we simply reach out in prayer and touch the hem of Jesus' garment. Today, He is still healing those who touch Him with their hearts.

1. What are in the *phylacteries* that some Orthodox Jews wrap on their heads and arms? _____

_____

2. Wearing the *phylacteries* are in observance of what commandment? _____

_____

3. How many tassels are typically around the fringe of a Jewish prayer shawl, and what do they represent?

_____

_____

4. What did Jesus say to the woman who touched the hem of his shawl? _____

_____

Day 25 — *Laughing at Life*

Of course, Christianity should be taken seriously. But shouldn't we be able to laugh, like Jesus did?

If God is really in control, we might as well enjoy life, instead of taking it so seriously. Jesus had a free and humorous way of teaching important truths. He loved to laugh and poke fun.

Why can't we do the same?

1. What is one of the primary fish caught in the Sea of Galilee commonly called, and how did it get its name?

_____

_____

2. What is one of the reasons Jesus spent so much time near the Sea of Galilee? _____

_____

3. Where was "home" to Jesus once He left Nazareth, and what happened there, more than in any other place? _____

_____

Day 24 — *Rock and Sand*

In Matthew 7, Jesus told the parable of two house builders. One was a wise man who built his house upon a rock, and the other a foolish man who built his house upon the sand. The house that was built upon rock withstood all kinds of weather, while the house that was built upon sand fell.

Have you built your life on solid rock or sinking sand? If you haven't built your house upon the rock—Jesus— then do so now, so that your foundation is unshakeable when the storms of life come.

1. What is a wadi? _____

_____

2. When the rains come in the desert, what happens in the wadis? _____

_____

3. What parable did Jesus use when closing out His Sermon on the Mount? _____

_____

4. Where does Jesus say the wise man builds his house? _____

5. Who built St. George's Monastery? _____

_____

Day 23 — *The Kingdom of God*

The Jews of Jesus' day were trained to love and respect the Law of God. They believed that the kingdom of God was nationalistic and that the coming Messiah would establish a military, political, and geographical kingdom, as in the time of David.

But when Jesus spoke of the kingdom of God, He was not talking about building a nation; rather, He was announcing His spiritual rule on Earth. Jesus came to destroy Satan's rule by deliberately challenging Satan on his own ground.

1. What is the number one subject of the Gospels?

_____

2. In the early days of Jesus' earthy ministry, what three things did He spend most of His time doing?

_____

_____

3. The only portion of the original Temple in Jerusalem that remains today is called what? _____

_____

4. How did Jesus tell His disciples to demonstrate that the King, the Messiah, had come to Earth? _____

_____

Day 22 — *The Sabbath*

In Israel, everything changes on the Sabbath—the Jewish holy day that extends from sunset Friday evening through sunset Saturday. Keeping and remembering the Sabbath is important. Even more important, however, is man's relationship with the Lord of the Sabbath.

1. What does the Hebrew word *Shabbat* mean? _____

_____

2. Which commandment teaches us to remember the Sabbath? _____

3. When does the Sabbath begin and end each week?

_____

4. How does the Bible say that we can make the Sabbath holy? _____

_____

5. How did Jesus respond to the Pharisees when they complained He was not honoring the Sabbath? _____

_____

Day 21 — *Community Life*

Community was important to the New Testament church, and it is important to modern-day Israel. Following the War of Independence in 1948, many new *kibbutzim* were started, as thousands of Jews arrived in Israel from all over the world. On a kibbutz, the people live and work together as a community.

1. What is a kibbutz? _____

_____

2. What does the Greek word *koinonia* mean in the Bible? _____

_____

3. Where in the Scriptures is the *koinonia* of the Church described? _____

_____

4. What happened in Israel in 1908? _____

_____

Day 20 — *Jesus the Man*

Although He was God incarnate, Jesus knew what it was like to put in a hard day's work.

Throughout His life on Earth, He also experienced the trials and tribulations common to mankind. He experienced discouragement and pain—including the excruciating physical pain of the cross.

Jesus was God become man. He knew what it was like to work, sweat, and be tired. As you worship Him, give thanks that He understands your problems. He has been where you are.

1. What is the Hebrew name for the Sea of Galilee, and why is it called that? _____

_____

2. Who built the city of Tiberius? _____

3. When Jesus left Nazareth to begin His public ministry, where did He first go? _____

_____

4. Why did Jesus eventually curse Capernaum? _____

_____

5. At what time did the disciples most like to fish on the Sea of Galilee? _____

Day 19 — *Dedicated Money*

During His earthly ministry, Jesus spent much of His time poking holes in religious balloons. The Pharisees of Jesus' day observed many of the traditions of men, and Jesus consistently called them out for it.

The law is only fulfilled when we love God with all our heart and love our neighbor as much as we love ourselves. Find someone to help. Use your time and/or money to bless someone else.

1. How did Jesus like to teach? _____

2. What did the Pharisees often accuse Jesus of doing?

_____

3. Jesus told the Pharisees that *Corban*—money dedicated to God—should be used for what purpose?

_____

4. According to Jesus, how did the Pharisees nullify the Word of God? _____

_____

5. When did Jesus say the true law of God—the law of love—is fulfilled? _____

_____

Day 18 — *Overcoming the Gates of Hell*

In Matthew 16:18, Jesus gave Peter a powerful promise: "And I tell you that you are Peter, and on this rock I will build My church."

Satan cannot overcome the authority of the Church. God's people have dominion over all of Satan's legions. What a powerful promise Jesus gave His Church! As Christians, we have full authority over Satan's government.

1. Where are the headwaters of the Jordan River? _____

_____

2. What Greek god is said to have been birthed there?

_____

3. What significant question did Jesus ask His disciples at Banias? _____

_____

4. What new name did Jesus give to Peter at Banias?

_____

5. What does the ancient Greek word for church, *Ecclesia*, literally mean? _____

_____

Day 17 — *Repentance and Confession*

Why do so many Christians consider sin an antiquated concept? Many in our Western culture consider guilt a disabling emotion.

Even though acknowledging guilt for our sins is never easy, it was Jesus who said that sin needs to be forgiven, because it damages the sinner.

God's nature is to forgive and forget. Today, pause for a moment and seek out the Shepherd. Confess your sin and receive God's forgiveness.

1. What is the item found on many Jewish doorposts, and what is in it? _____

_____

2. In Jewish tradition, how were sins forgiven? _____

_____

3. Instead of sacrifice, what does God desire of us?

_____

_____

Day 16 — *Have Mercy on Me*

When traveling through Jericho on His way to
Jerusalem, Jesus certainly had a lot on His mind—
namely, the fact that He was on His way to His
crucifixion.

Yet, Jesus did not refuse the cry for help from a blind
beggar, Bartimaeus, who implored Jesus to heal him.
Although He was on His way to death, Jesus took time
to stop and heal the man.

Can we be like Jesus? Reach out today and touch
someone in need, regardless of the difficulty of your
own circumstances.

1. What is so unique about the city of Jericho? _____

_____

2. How old is the ancient city of Jericho? _____

3. Why is the Jericho Road so notorious? _____

_____

4. Which of Jesus' parables takes place along the
Jericho Road? _____

_____

Day 15 — *Determination*

Jesus was spending time in the little town of Betharba when word came that His friend, Lazarus, was dying. His disciples wanted Him to stay put. Traveling back into Judea, they said, would be dangerous. But Jesus was determined to go *where* the Father directed, *when* the Father directed—even if it meant facing certain death.

1. What were the names of Lazarus' two sisters? _____

_____

2. What information was Jesus referring to when He told Peter, "Only God can reveal that kind of information to you"? _____

_____

3. In Jesus' day, what kind of Messiah were most Jews expecting? _____

_____

_____

Day 14 — *Life After Death*

In Bethany, Jesus had something bigger in mind than healing His old friend, Lazarus. It was nearing the time for His crucifixion, and Jesus knew that He was going to lay down His life as a ransom for the world. By raising Lazarus from the dead, Jesus confirmed that He was, indeed, the Son of God.

If we link our lives with Jesus, allowing the Spirit which raised Him from the dead to come and live in us, then we, too, will live as Jesus lives!

1. Who first asked the question, "If a man dies, will he live again?" _____

2. What town did Lazarus and his sisters live in? _____

_____

3. Why did Jesus raise Lazarus from the dead? _____

_____

4. What is the only guarantee for eternal life after death? _____

_____

_____

Day 13 — *L'Chaim – To Life*

When the body of Lazarus was placed in the tomb and a heavy stone was rolled over the entrance, everyone believed they had seen their brother and friend for the last time.

But when Jesus' authoritative voice commanded Lazarus to "come forth," suddenly, there was life. With one phrase, all of the processes of death were reversed. Lazarus' body returned to life with a simple word from God.

Do you have life? Are you free in the Spirit, or are you bound in the grave clothes of dead tradition? Jesus stands today at your tomb, calling you to *L'Chaim!*

1. How were the poor buried in the days of Jesus? ___

_____

2. Approximately how deep was Lazarus' tomb? ____

_____

3. How long was Lazarus in the tomb? _____

_____

4. What does the Jewish term *L'Chaim* mean? _____

_____

Day 12 — *The Holy Spirit*

The night before He was crucified, Jesus told His followers that they would do greater things on the earth than He had done. After His resurrection, He told them to wait for the gift that God had promised them—the Holy Spirit—for the power to do these greater things.

In Acts 2, while the disciples were gathered in an upper room, a mighty wind rushed through the house. The Bible says that in that moment, the apostles were filled with the Holy Spirit. They began to speak in other tongues and experienced new boldness and power to share the gospel with the world.

Because we are His followers, Jesus wants to empower us by His Spirit to go into all the world and tell others about Him.

1. When was Jesus arrested? _____

_____

2. Who sentenced Jesus to death? _____

3. What is the name of the path Jesus took as He carried His own cross to Calvary? _____

_____

4. How many believers were in the upper room when the Holy Spirit filled them? _____

Day 11 — *Filled with the Spirit*

A week before His crucifixion, Jesus told His disciples the parable of the ten virgins who went out to meet the bridegroom. Five were wise and brought extra oil for their lamps, while five were foolish and did not.

When the bridegroom finally came, only five of the virgins were prepared. The door of the wedding feast was shut, and the five unprepared virgins were shut out.

It's not enough to simply belong to a church or even to pray. We need reserve oil. We need to be filled with the Holy Spirit.

1. What signs did Jesus say would accompany the end of times? _____

_____

2. How many bridesmaids, or "virgins," are in the parable of the wedding feast? _____

3. How many wise bridesmaids had reserve oil when the bridegroom showed up? _____

4. What does the reserve oil represent? _____

_____

Day 10 — *Who Killed Jesus?*

The question is still asked in Israel today: Who killed Jesus?

Was it the Roman soldiers who drove the nails into His hands and feet and raised the cross, where He hung until He died? Was it Pontius Pilate, who sentenced Him to death? Was it the Jews and their religious leaders who brought Him before Pilate to be sentenced? Or was it Judas, who betrayed Him?

1. Who killed Jesus? _____

_____

2. What is the compelling force that draws men and women to God? _____

_____

3. What three languages were used for the words written above Jesus on His cross? _____

_____

Day 9 — *The Power of Jesus*

Jesus' execution was a result of personal choice. He was not a victim of an evil empire, nor was He broken or defeated. Even on the cross, there was never a moment that He was not in full control.

We should give thanks for Jesus and give our lives completely to Him, so that we can have the same victory over Satan that He did.

1. What option has God given each of us? _____

_____

_____

2. Where was Jesus when He made His final determination to voluntarily go to the cross to atone for our sins? _____

_____

3. In the history of the struggle between God and Satan, has there ever been a time when God was not in control? _____

Day 8 — *The Peace of Jerusalem*

Across the centuries, Jerusalem, the City of David, has been destroyed and rebuilt time and time again. Regardless of the destruction, Jerusalem keeps being resurrected, like God's creations are always resurrected. As a result, the city is a marvelous mixture of old and new.

The psalmist says we are to "pray for the peace of Jerusalem." What brings true peace? Not military or political power. Not money. Not fame. Not hedonistic pleasure. These things bring anxiety—and death. But if you invite Jesus, the living Lord, into your life, He brings peace.

1. In the Psalms, how did David refer to Jerusalem?

_____

2. According to the prophet Ezekiel, where would the glory of God be manifest? _____

_____

3. Where did Jesus tell His disciples the kingdom of God was? _____

_____

Day 7 — Palm Sunday — *Hosanna*

The night before Jesus rode into Jerusalem, He stayed at the home of Mary, Martha, and Lazarus.

Rising early the next morning, His disciples must have wondered what was in store for this particular day. Why ride a donkey through the streets of Jerusalem?

Jesus was calling for the world to make a choice. Are we among those who are willing to stand and wave palm leaves, but not to stand with Jesus in the end? Or are we willing to give our lives to Him as Lord and Savior?

1. What point in Jesus' life is considered the "watershed"—the pivotal point of no turning back?

_____

2. What did the Jewish rabbis in Jesus' time believe was involved in the raising of the dead? _____

_____

3. Why did the people of Jerusalem swarm out to meet Jesus on what is now called Palm Sunday? _____

_____

4. What has the Church come to call the last week of Jesus' life on Earth (the last week of Lent)? _____

_____

Day 6 — *The Golden Gate*

Prior to His death and resurrection, Jesus entered Jerusalem through the Golden Gate into the temple grounds. There is deep significance in Jesus' decision to enter through that gate, which was reserved for use by the high priest.

Jesus was and is our High Priest, the one who atoned for our sins.

The gate has since been closed up with bricks. Many believe Christ will use the same gate when He enters the city of Jerusalem again, after His Second Coming. The bricks are one more example of man's feeble attempts to hinder the will of God.

1. What did Jesus say when He was angered by the merchants in the Temple? _____

_____

2. Which gate did Jesus use to enter Jerusalem, and why is that significant? _____

_____

3. What have Muslims and some Jews done on the Mount of Olives slope in front of the Golden Gate?

_____

_____

Day 5 — *Lord of Life*

During the final week of His life, Jesus repeatedly told His disciples of the events that were soon to take place. Still, the disciples didn't fully understand what they were about to witness, because they did not fully understand what type of Messiah Jesus really was.

Understand what it is to be known as a child of God! Don't simply recognize Him as your Savior; receive Him into your heart as the Lord of your life.

1. What was the last meal called that Jesus ate with His disciples before His arrest? _____

2. Who arranged for the arrest of Jesus? _____

_____

3. Who was the traitor amongst Jesus' followers who betrayed Him to the authorities? _____

_____

4. What does Passover signify? _____

_____

_____

Day 4 — *The Upper Room*

After the Passover meal on the night before His crucifixion, Jesus took a basin and a towel and washed the feet of His disciples. He did this to show them His desire that they serve one another.

Next to the cross, nothing gives us a more dramatic picture of what God wants us to be than the towel and the basin.

1. During the Passover meal, what did Jesus say the bread and cup of wine represented? _____

_____

2. What did Jesus do immediately following the Passover meal? _____

3. What new commandment did He give following the washing of His disciples' feet? _____

_____

4. What does the act of washing of the feet symbolize to us? _____

_____

Day 3 — Maundy Thursday — *Tough Decisions*

In the Garden of Gethsemane, Jesus knew what was coming, but He prayed to His Father anyway. Would God protect Him from an agonizing death on the cross?

Luke 22:42 says that Jesus prayed, "Father, if You are willing, remove this cup from Me. Nevertheless, not My will, but Yours be done." Jesus knew the answer. To fulfill His mission, He had to go to the cross.

Most of us will not be faced with such an excruciating, life-or-death decision in our lifetime. Nevertheless, we should always pray that God's will, not ours, be done, in everything we say and do.

1. What (or who) did Jesus promise to send into the world following His death on the cross? _____

2. What was the name of the valley that Jesus crossed through to enter the Garden of Gethsemane? _____

_____

3. Jesus prophesied that Peter would disown Him three times before what happened? _____

_____

4. Which three disciples did Jesus take with Him to pray in the garden? _____

_____

Day 2 — *Via Dolorosa*

According to tradition, the Via Dolorosa in Jerusalem is the path that Jesus walked as He carried His cross to Calvary. No one knows for certain, since most of the surrounding buildings were knocked down when the city was destroyed by Rome in 70 A.D.

Flogged and adorned with a crown of thorns, Jesus was whipped and brutalized all the way to the cross. Yet, He was still consumed with love for mankind—including those who were, at that moment, placing nails in His hands and feet.

1. What does "Via Dolorosa" literally mean? _____

_____

2. How many "stations" have historians identified where significant things happened to Jesus as He made His way to Calvary? _____

3. What was the judgement hall of Pilate called? _____

_____

4. Who was Simon from Cyrene? _____

_____

5. Through which gate did Jesus exit the city on the way to Calvary? _____

Day 1 — *Calvary*

Why did Jesus have to die? Romans 5:6-8 gives us a concise answer: "When we were still powerless, Christ died for the ungodly. . . God demonstrated his own love for us in that while we were still sinners, Christ died for us."

Jesus died so that we might live eternally with Him, with God. His death opened the door back to God. All we have to do is let Him come in and be Lord of our lives.

1. What is the hill of Calvary also known as? _____

_____

2. How long had the Jews in Israel lived without a prophet? _____

3. How does Paul, in Romans, say we can be saved?

_____

_____

_____

Easter Sunday — *The Empty Tomb*

Israel is a land of graves. Tombstones seem to be on every hillside. But only one grave is empty. All the others are filled with the bones of dead men and women.

Jesus alone has risen from the grave. And because He lives, God has given eternal life to all who believe and confess with their mouths that Jesus is indeed Lord.

The story of God's love for us does not end with the Crucifixion. Nor does it end with Easter. It only begins there. Just like those early disciples, each of us has been commanded to seek and receive the baptism of the Holy Spirit, so that we, too, can be empowered to go into all the world and tell others about our risen Lord.

1. What is the symbol of Jesus greatest conquest—victory over death? _____

_____

2. Three days after the Crucifixion, what did the women return to the grave of Jesus to do? _____

_____

3. Who said, "Why do you look for the living among the dead? He is not here. He is risen"? _____

_____

Jamie Buckingham

Answers to Questions

Day 49 — 1. Spring; 2. The 40 days Jesus spent in the desert after His baptism; 3. The last Sunday of Epiphany - the Sunday before the beginning of Lent - 50 days before Easter; 4. Preparation for the celebration of the Resurrection. The weekdays are considered fasting days; Sundays are a day of celebration. As followers of Jesus, we don't have to wait for Easter to celebrate His resurrection.

Day 48 — 1. 1947; 2. Large portions of the Old Testament dating back to the 1st century; 3. Only a truly good person is truly free; 4. John the Baptist; 5. It was part of God's plan for His life; 6. It is a description of the coming Messiah.

Day 47 — 1. Sinai Desert and Wilderness of Zin; 2. Israel took the Sinai Peninsula from Egypt; 3. The Six-Day War, when Israel repelled attacks by the joined forces of Egypt, Syria and Jordan, and captured the city of Jerusalem; 4. Come to Jesus and He will give us rest, for "My yoke is easy and My burden is light."

Day 46 — 1. Ash Wednesday; 2. Repentance, humility, fasting and praying; 3. The Western Wall, or Wailing Wall, the site of the original Temple; 4. 900 years; 5. Muslims; 6. The very rock upon which Abraham was about to sacrifice his son, Isaac; 7. In a way not obvious to man, but only as before God.

Day 45 — 1. For no other reason than the fact God considers them the chosen ones; 2. They began to plant trees, to replace the ones destroyed by the Turks in their attempt to wipe out the Jews and destroy the land; 3. Rain; 4. Job.

Day 44 — 1. Herod the Great; 2. He was Jewish, though a renegade Jew; 3. Micah; 4. Three, (a) Herod Philipus, (b) Herod Antipas, (c) Herod Archelaus.

Day 43 — 1. In a shepherd's field outside Bethlehem at the time of Jesus' birth; 2. Messenger; 3. (a) Minister to God around His throne; (b) minister to humans; (c) as messengers from God to humans; 4. They may be "angels unawares"; 5. "Why do you seek the living among the dead? He is risen."

Day 42 — 1. 1,300 feet below sea level; 2. The Judean Wilderness for 40 days; 3. His baptism; 4. The Holy Spirit came on Him like a dove, and He was filled with the Holy Spirit; 5. (a) Rule over an earthly kingdom based on materialism; (b) superior power over humans; (c) magical works not of God.

Day 41 — 1. The anointed one; 2. Christ; 3. Free them from earthly tyranny and bondage and make them a great nation to rule over the entire Earth; 4. Safed at 2,600 feet above sea level; 5. The "Throne of the Messiah"; 6. 700 years.

Day 40 — 1. James, John and Peter; 2. They wanted to build monuments to the men; 3. By simply commanding that the spirit leave the child; 4. To give us abundant life here on Earth.

Day 39 — 1. On the north shore of the Sea of Galilee; 2. His disciples; 3. Happy, filled with joy; 4. Service to others, comfort, meekness, righteousness, mercy, peace and persecution; 5. Because we are different, followers of Christ, and not of this world; 6. Safed.

Day 38 — 1. Capernaum; 2. The Golan Heights; 3. Michael and Gabriel; 4. They are former angels banished with Lucifer/Satan; 5. The Holy Spirit.

Day 37 — 1. 4,000; 2. They swarmed into a herd of pigs, who then flung themselves off a cliff into the sea and drowned; 3. Powers of the dark world and spiritual forces of evil in the heavenlies; 4. We are to command them to leave in the name of Jesus.

Day 36 — 1. "The living death"; 2. They were to be banished and declared spiritually dead and unclean; 3. He overrode the Law of Moses with the law of love, and the laws of nature with the law of healing.

Day 35 — 1. Nicodemus; 2. The Sanhedrin; 3. You must repent of your sinful nature and die to self; 4. By surrendering to Jesus and asking Him to take control of your life.

Day 34 — 1. Three years; 2. The end of Jewish independence until 1948; 3. He often "withdrew to lonely places to pray," into the hills; 4. You talking to God and God talking to you.

Day 33 — 1. 100 miles; 2. Mt. Carmel; 3. The end of the three-year drought; 4. Mt. Sinai; 5. Sent angels to minister to him.

Day 32 — 1. God's blessing; 2. Times when God reveals Himself, and the arrival of life; 3. The one that received Jesus after His resurrection, and the one in which He will return at His Second Coming.

Day 31 — 1. Tourism; 2. Being a shepherd. He called Himself "the Good Shepherd"; 3. By considering others better than ourselves and giving our lives to those less fortunate than we are; 4. Giving herself to the "lambs" of Jesus' flock and feeding the sheep.

Day 30 — 1. To keep an eye on the workers, to protect the harvest from thieves and wild animals, and to see if the enemy was coming; 2. The coming Messiah; 3. One who manages, one who is in charge, an overseer; 4. To take care of what God has placed in our realm of responsibility, to protect it from the enemy, to see that the harvest is taken in, to give back to the Owner His rightful share.

Day 29 — 1. A great storm arose and Jesus calmed the seas; 2. 660 feet; 3. With authority; 4. To take charge over something with God's authority; 5. When he attempts to stop us from doing what God has called us to do.

Day 28 — 1. Herod beheaded him; 2. 5,000; 3. Do what you can with what you have, in faith, and God will do the multiplication; 4. Two fish and five loaves of bread; 5. 12 full baskets.

Day 27 — 1. Herod the Great; over 12 years; 2. The Romans would not tolerate the worship of any god other than Caesar; 3. They are an everlasting memorial to the power of Christ.

Day 26 — 1. Scripture passages written on small pieces of paper; 2. Deut. 6 says to "bind the commands of the Lord on your arm and your forehead"; 3. 613—one for each of the laws of the Torah, the first five books of the Bible; 4. "Daughter, your faith has healed you."

Day 25 — 1. "St. Peter's fish," because Simon Peter found a coin in the mouth of one of the fish; 2. He wanted to be near His disciples, who were fishermen; 3. Capernaum, the city where Jesus performed more miracles than any other place.

Day 24 — 1. A dry riverbed in the Sinai; 2. They become filled with rushing water and cause dangerous flash floods; 3. The parable of two houses, one built on rock and one built on sand; 4. On the rock, not the sand; 5. Greek monks, hundreds of years ago.

Day 23 — 1. The kingdom of God; 2. Teaching in the synagogues, preaching the good news of the kingdom, and healing every sickness and disease; 3. The Western Wall, also known as the Wailing Wall; 4. Heal the sick, raise the dead, cleanse those with leprosy, drive out demons; "freely you have received, freely give."

Day 22 — 1. Rest; 2. The 4th Commandment; 3. Sundown on Friday through sundown on Saturday; 4. Remember it/observe it; 5. "The Sabbath was made for man, not man for the Sabbath."

Day 21— 1. A farming or industrial community in Israel, where people live and work and hold all things in common; 2. Christian community or fellowship; 3. The second chapter of Acts; 4. The first immigrants arrived in Israel and formed the first kibbutz.

Day 20 — 1. Kinneret, which means "harp." The Sea of Galilee is shaped like a shepherd's harp; 2. Herod Antipas; 3. Capernaum; 4. The people refused to respond to His ministry; 5. At night.

Day 19 — 1. Through the use of parables; 2. Breaking the religious laws, and being a blasphemous heretic; 3. Help people and not line the pockets of religious leaders; 4. By their traditions. By forcing people to serve the rules rather than having the rules serve us; 5. When we love God with all our heart and we love our neighbor as ourselves.

Day 18 — 1. Banias, in the Golan Heights; 2. Pan, the god of nature. Pan was half-man, half-goat; 3. "Who do you say I am?"; 4. Petra, the Greek word for rock; 5. "The called out ones."

Day 17 — 1. A mezuzah. It holds a paper with a scripture written on it; 2. Through a blood sacrifice; 3. A repentant and contrite heart.

Day 16 — 1. It is 800 feet below sea level, the lowest city in the world; 2. 5,000 years; 3. It stretches far into the Judean wilderness and is abounding with wild animals and thieves; 4. The Good Samaritan.

Day 15 — 1. Mary and Martha; 2. That Jesus is the Messiah, the Son of the living God; 3. A thundering prophet or a military leader to overthrow Roman oppression.

Day 14 — 1. Job; 2. Bethany; 3. So no one could doubt that He was indeed the son of God; 4. Accepting Jesus as Lord and Savior.

Day 13 — 1. The body was wrapped in a cloth, laid on the ground and covered with stones to keep the animals away; 2. About 30 feet; 3. About four days; 4. "To Life!"

Day 12 — 1. Thursday night, the final night of Passover; 2. The Roman governor, Pontius Pilate; 3. Via Dolorosa, The Way of Sorrows; 4. 120.

Day 11 — 1. There would be wars and rumors of wars; people would grow more wicked; many of those in the church would become humanistic and fall away. No one knows when the end of time will take place; 2. Ten; 3. Five; 4. Being filled with the Holy Spirit.

Day 10 — 1. No one. Jesus voluntarily laid down His life for us; 2. The power of the Holy Spirit; 3. Hebrew, Latin and Greek.

Day 9 — 1. We have the power of choice, to choose God or not choose Him; 2. The Garden of Gethsemane; 3. No.

Day 8 — 1. "The mother of mankind"; 2. The Mount of Olives outside Jerusalem; 3. Jesus said, "The kingdom of God is within you."

Day 7 — 1. The day He raised Lazarus from the dead; 2. Magic, or conjuring, not miracle power from God; 3. They expected Him to announce His Messiahship and set up an earthy kingdom to save them from the Romans; 4. The Passion Week.

Day 6 — 1. "You have turned God's house of prayer into a den of thieves"; 2. The Golden Gate. It was reserved for priests to use. Jesus is our high priest, the one who atones for our sin; 3. Buried their dead, believing it will prevent Jesus from entering the gate upon His return.

Day 5 — 1. The Passover Meal; 2. The Jewish religious leaders; 3. Judas; 4. It commemorates the time when the Jews were slaves in Egypt and the angel of death passed over their houses, because their doorposts were marked with the blood of the lamb.

Day 4 — 1. His body, broken for us, and His blood, shed for us; 2. He washed the feet of His disciples; 3. "You should love one another"; 4. That we are to be a people who serve one another.

Day 3 — 1. The Holy Spirit; 2. The Kedron Valley; 3. Before the rooster crowed; 4. Peter, James and John.

Day 2 — 1. The Way of Sorrows; 2. Fourteen; 3. The Praetorium; 4. The man the Roman soldiers pulled from the crowd to carry Jesus' cross; 5. The Gate of Judgement.

Day 1 — 1. Golgotha, "the place of the skull"; 2. 400 years; 3. "If you confess with your mouth, Jesus is Lord, and believe in your heart that God raised him from the dead, you will be saved" (Romans 10:9).

Easter Day — 1. The empty tomb; 2. Anoint His body with spices; 3. The angel in the empty tomb.

ABOUT JAMIE BUCKINGHAM

A master storyteller, Jamie Buckingham delighted millions around the world both in person and in print. He was recognized as one of the key Christian authors from the early 1970s until his death in 1992.

As a distinguished Bible teacher with graduate degrees in English Literature and Theology, Jamie was respected among liturgical, evangelical, and Pentecostal Christians. He was considered a close friend and confidant of many key Christians of the late 20th century.

Jamie was more than an author of books. He was an award-winning columnist for *Charisma Magazine,* editor at *Guideposts Magazine* and editor-in-chief of *Ministries Today Magazine.* A popular conference speaker, he was recognized as one of America's foremost authorities on the Sinai and Israel. He wrote and produced more than 100 video teachings on location in the Holy Land.

Jamie was founding pastor of the Tabernacle Church, an interdenominational congregation in Melbourne, Florida, where he served for 25 years. He lived in a rural area on the east coast of Florida with his wife, Jackie, surrounded by five married children and 14 grandchildren.

For more information on Jamie Buckingham, please visit www.JamieBuckinghamMinistries.com.

Books by Jamie Buckingham

Risky Living
A Way Through the Wilderness
Where Eagles Soar
Coping With Criticism
The Nazarene
Jesus World (a novel)
Bible People Like Me
Miracle Power
Parable of Jesus
Into the Glory
The Truth Will Set You Free . . . But First It Will Make You Miserable
The Last Word
Spiritual Maturity
A Spirit-Led Life
The Brightness of Your Rising (compiled sermons by Jamie)
Armed for Spiritual Warfare
Power for Living
Summer of Miracles
Pits Along the Road to Glory (previously unpublished)

Booklets from teachings by Jamie Buckingham

God is in Control
When Your Prayers Go Unanswered
Senior Saints
Laughing at Life
Unproductive Seasons
When You Are Born Ugly
Essentials for Hearing God
How to Get Ready to Die
Activating Angels through Prayer
Healing for Today
Perseverance and God's Faithfulness
The Weights of Life
Thanksgiving in the Pit

ABOUT BRUCE BUCKINGHAM

Bruce Buckingham is the eldest son of Jamie Buckingham. Following his retirement from NASA in 2013, Bruce formed a not-for-profit corporation, Risky Living Ministries, dedicated to preserving the works and teachings of his father. He then began the long process of collecting and digitizing Jamie's teachings and out-of-print publications. Over the past several years, Bruce has collected over 950 cassette tapes and reel-to-reel audio teachings of Jamie's sermons from all over the world. He is in the process of editing those recordings and putting them on the website www.JamieBuckinghamMinistries.com.

In addition, Risky Living Ministries, under Bruce's direction, has republished over 30 of Jamie's books and video devotional workbooks. They are available once again, after being out of print for decades, in paperback, e-book, and audio book formats.

While at NASA, Bruce severed as the "voice of NASA launch control" during the space shuttle program. He later became Strategic Communications Director at Kennedy Space Center, Florida, prior to his retirement.

Bruce recently published his own first novel, *The Last Snowman in Paris*, as well as a book of his short stories.

For more about Bruce Buckingham please visit:
http://bbuckingham321.wixsite.com/brucebuckingham

For more of Jamie Buckingham's books, teachings and video devotionals, or if you would like additional copies of this study guide, go to:

www.JamieBuckinghamMinistries.com

Other video devotionals by Jamie Buckingham include:

10 Miracles of Jesus
10 Bible People Like Me
10 Parables of Jesus
Journey to Spiritual Maturity
Armed for Spiritual Warfare

You can also us on Facebook.

Risky Living Ministries, Inc.

www.RLMin.com